LEARN THE VALUE OF

# Understanding Others

by ELAINE P. GOLEY

Illustrated by Debbie Crocker

ROURKE ENTERPRISES, INC.
VERO BEACH, FL 32964

**Library of Congress Cataloging-in-Publication Data**

Goley, Elaine P., 1949–
    Learn the value of understanding others.

    Summary: Depicts situations that demonstrate
the meaning and importance of understanding others.
    1. Empathy—Juvenile literature.  [1. Empathy.
2. Conduct of life]  I. Title.  II. Title:
Understanding others.
BF575.E55G67  1987      158'.2        87-16324
ISBN 0-86592-382-5

# Understanding
# Others

Do you know about **understanding others?**

**Understanding others** is knowing your mom
loves you, even when she scolds you.

Knowing others can't always do the same things
you can, is **understanding others.**

You're **understanding others** when you know that your baby brother cries a lot because he can't talk yet.

Knowing that your friend is just like you
even though his skin is a different color,
is **understanding others.**

Letting someone be by herself when she wants
to be, is **understanding others.**

You're **understanding others** when you know that even your big sister can have problems.

**Understanding others** is knowing that your
neighbor can't play with you on Saturday because
he goes to a different church from yours.

When you try not to hurt someone's feelings,
you're **understanding others.**

You're **understanding others** when you give a flower to someone who's sad.

**Understanding others** is telling your friends not
to tease somebody because he's different.

If your friend is sad, try showing you **understand**
by flying a kite with him.

When you speak louder so that Grandma can hear you better, you're **understanding others**.

Letting someone take her time coming down the slide because she's a little afraid, is **understanding others.**

**Understanding others** is letting someone share
your bike because he doesn't have one of his own.

You're **understanding others** when you put Max in the yard because your friend is afraid of dogs.

Listening when your friend has something to tell you, is **understanding others.**

**Understanding others** is putting yourself in
someone else's place so that you know how it feels.

# Understanding Others

"I don't want to go the movies," said Patty. "Leave me alone."

"What's wrong with you?" asked Rosa.

"Nothing," said Patty. She hung up the phone and began to cry.

"Mom, Dad, Patty was very angry with me on the phone this morning," said Rosa.

"Well, her dad doesn't have a job anymore," said Mr. Garcia. "The Burkes don't have much money. Patty is probably worried."

"Now I know why Patty was upset," said Rosa. "She didn't have money for the movies. I didn't spend all the money from my allowance. I'm sure there's enough for two movie tickets."

"Where are you going?" asked Mrs. Garcia.

"To the movies with my best friend, Patty," said Rosa as she ran out the door.

What do you think Rosa will say to Patty? How do you show you **understand others?**

# Understanding Others

"How are you feeling, Randy?" asked Tyrone. "Is your leg any better?"

"The operation helped," said Randy. "But I still limp a little."

"Are you going on the Scout hike next month?" asked Tyrone. "It's going to be fun."

"Oh, I don't think so. I'll slow everyone down and spoil the fun," said Randy.

"If you get tired, I'll help you," said Tyrone. "I'll carry your pack."

"Well, OK," said Randy.

On his way home from Randy's house, Tyrone saw his friend Patrick.

"Going on the hike?" asked Patrick.

"Sure. Randy is coming too," said Tyrone.

"What?" said Patrick. "Randy walks too slowly. If he goes, I'm staying home."

Which boy showed he **understood others?**

How can you show **understanding** to people who are different from you?